CW00971556

The Cat's Guide to Human Behavior

The Cat's Guide to Human Behavior

as told to Xina Marie Uhl

XC Publishing

BISAC subject headings:

HUM009000   HUMOR / Topic / Animals
HUM007000   HUMOR / Form / Parodies
PET003000   PETS / Cats / General

XC Publishing
653 Calle Pensamiento
Thousand Oaks, CA 91360
www.XCPublishing.net

Introduction

Y ou'll figure it out soon, if you haven't already. No matter how much effort you put forth during the process, choosing the right human for you was just the beginning. Now you must train your human to behave properly. This can be quite the challenge! However, it is well worth the time and energy involved. After all, how will your person know how to keep you happy and fulfilled if you don't teach them?

This guide will help you understand not only the strange quirks and baffling habits of your human, but also the sometimes confounding terrain they inhabit. It is not enough that you understand the humans' behaviors, however. You must also know how to respond to them. Fortunately, I have compiled this guide based on the wisdom of the wise felines that have gone before you. You hold in your paws if not a holy book, then at the very least an indispensable textbook on life. Never forget that you have a long tradition to follow. Keeping humans in their proper place will make your life both happy and complete.

Chapter One

Your Domain

Whan shared with humans, your den is not only your castle, it is also a wondrous and sometimes frightening maze of adventure. Here you'll find many nooks and crannies to explore, many dark spaces to rest in: boxes and doors and bowls and basins. High, flat cliffs and carpeted fields. Soft, warm sleeping platforms. Loud, squawking boxes. Roaring monsters that slide along the floor. Hills and valleys of fabric. Strange small devices which emit light and noise. Captivating, unfamiliar, scrumptious smells. Sources of heat and light, of cold and liquid.

Here is also where your human spends much of their days and most every night, sleeping, eating, grooming, chattering, attempting to mate, or staring mindlessly at a box on the wall. You will learn very quickly that humans do many puzzling things and have many strange, inexplicable habits. Sometimes you can train your human to bow to your will easily; other times, however, you must simply endure until they cease their rebellion and properly acquiesce. This guide can help you decide the best course of action.

Sleeping

The sheer number of hours a day you spend sleeping dwarfs any other activity. Therefore, it is important to understand how human sleep patterns differ from your own. Humans suffer from hyperactivity disorders that limits their sleeping hours to a mere 7 to 10 per night. In extreme cases, some humans regularly make do with six hours or less. Once asleep, however, they can be difficult to wake during the darkest hours. Furthermore, when you do manage to awaken them, they often simply burrow deeper in the fluff they surround themselves with and fall back asleep. Other times they may eject you from their sleeping platform entirely. Because of this, many felines simply adjust their sleeping hours to match that of their humans.

Occasionally, however, it is necessary to awaken them in order to show them who's boss. An uppity human can never be a truly effective companion. Such is more appropriate for that silly, slobbering tail-wagger known as the dog.

Your own sleeping routine will sometimes be interrupted when humans, longing for your presence, lift you bodily and place you on their laps. The only sensible response to this is to hiss and retreat under the bed. Humans cannot be allowed to treat your sacred person in such a fashion, lest it become a habit.

However, when you desire to sleep, gain warmth, or exhibit affection, do not hesitate to approach your human. Lie down either on the human or in their direct line of sight, especially if said human is bending forward at the shining screen, making tapping motions with their fingers, or holding up and staring at large crinkling sheets of paper.

THINGS TO TRY

Effective means of waking your human include (1) Pouncing on their feet with claws extended. This may be performed with or without added playful biting. (2)

Executing your monthly cardiovascular activities up and down the drapes in their sleeping hovel. (3) Walking, sitting, lying, and/or kneading your claws on their heads and faces. (4) Calling to them in a loud, forceful, and repeated manner, especially if you are hungry.

Males and Females

In general, you will find that human females are more amenable to you than the males. Female voices get even higher when they see you. They cannot resist stroking your fur and scratching your head. They coo and smile and generally treat you with more honor than the adult males. Adult males, like tom cats, spend so much of their time attempting to mate with females, or in some cases, with other males, that they usually prefer stupider and more agreeable companions, like guinea pigs or cockroaches.

Young males, however, are the exception to this rule. Children of both sexes, once they grow out of the loud and annoying phase where they lie around and scream, or toddle around and scream, are generally fine companions. They will spend much time gently petting you or telling you their problems. When they mishandle you, they are usually easily disciplined with scratches or hisses. Adult females are usually vigilant when their children are around us, unlike adult males who seem to spend most of their time hunched and twitching over the glowing box screen we mentioned earlier or consuming salty, crunchy foods that they will on occasion offer to you if you stare at them long enough.

Although adult males seem disinclined to clean out your litter box or feed you the exact flavor of pulpy meat that you are accustomed to, they are preferred by some felines. This generally happens when another animal in the den sticks close to the female or when there is no female in the den. While adult males generally sweat more and fling garbage about the den more than the females, they are—when necessary— appropriate sources of heat and affection.

New Partners

When humans mate, they tend to live together even when the female is not in heat. Because of this, you may be present for the introduction of a new potential mate for your human. This can be an unsettling time, since the new person can cause great changes in the den, sometimes for the worse. In general, the introduction of a female to the den is a good thing for both you and the male. The female, as we have noted, usually worships you as you deserve, offering you tidbits and speaking pleasingly to you.

When your single female brings an unfamiliar male around, however, you may encounter difficulties. The male may disdain your company, fear your hold over the female, or step on you when staggering through the den after a night of feasting and/or coupling. In the event that the male does not show sufficient signs of respect on account of your superiority, you may need to take action. This can be accomplished in various ways. More effective methods include: leaping at him unexpectedly from atop the food box, doors, drapes, or shelves; climbing up his bare leg and scratching whatever dangly bits you encounter along the way; peeing on the windshield of his moveable den; and sinking your razor-sharp fangs into his nose and refusing to release them until his screams of pain become whimpers of terror and he runs off into the night, never to return.

Note: these techniques may also be employed towards unfriendly visitors, mean neighbors, or humans who get on your bad side for specific reasons, or, let's face it, no reasons whatsoever.

Chapter Two

Entertainment

Watching humans is always entertaining, as long as you sit in a dignified pose (feet in front, shoulders back, chin lifted) and do not blink. Ever. Some of the more nervous humans actually get up and flee the room when you do this. It can be a significant source of entertainment.

Getting Comfortable

Of course sleep will make up the majority of your leisure time, so be sure to put forth considerable effort to find the best possible sleeping arrangements. Most times you will want a soft, warm spot on one of the pieces of furniture that the humans so favor. However, sometimes that just won't do, especially when you wish to survey your domain from up high, and then nap for a few hours after the effort you expended to get up there. My favorite spots have been, variously: the top of the hard box filled with cold air and food items; inside a dark closet atop a stack of the fluffy pieces of cloth that humans use to wick water away from their hulking forms; or at the end of the humans' sleeping platform, an especially attractive place after I've managed to go outside and squelch the scent of humanity with a good roll in recently manured earth.

Odiferous items of various textures usually arrive in the humans' den in brown boxes of varying sizes, which are then flung aside in favor of whatever piece of junk the human has become besotted with. These are particularly comfortable spaces that can also serve a secondary function as chew toys. Beware, though, that you do not spend too much time in them, since humans cause them to disappear with distressing regularity.

Consider the case of Muck, a regal, gray, long-haired stud with haunting yellow eyes and fine black whiskers. He often reclined in the cool, smooth stone bowl of the tiny room in which humans splash water on themselves. The rounded shape of the bowl fit his form nicely, and he spent many happy hours luxuriating in his chosen space. However, his human companions, an elderly couple who evidently could not see well, had a disturbing habit of coming into the room, defecating or urinating, and then releasing the waterfall above Muck's head. Muck did the right thing by refusing to move despite the humans' entreaties to the contrary, leading to many long grooming sessions where he licked away the moisture that landed, unerringly, upon his forehead. Take this as a cautionary tale that while a resting place may seem ideal to you, your humans may have other, infuriating ideas.

The Active Life

Hunting is a favorite activity of most felines; in particular, the young who are just learning skills that may assist them in the future. If you are able to practice this skill outside the humans' den, you are lucky. Most of us must remain content with hunting inside the den: stalking waterfalls that run for mere moments at a time in the tiny water and elimination room and near the metal food box; pouncing upon stray strings hanging from the fabric humans wear on their bodies; dashing madly after stray bugs in order to snack upon them; and allowing your human to pet you three or four times before unexpectedly whipping around and sinking your fangs into their moist, hairless paws.

Humans enjoy producing toys for you, and watching as you bat at them, shred them, or in the case of that elusive red light dot, chase after them with manic glee. In all but the most exceptional circumstances, these will not satisfy you for long. Playing with fellow felines or, in cases of extremity, other lesser, furry denizens of your living space, is usually more enjoyable. Sometimes, if the denizen has wings, a play session can even end in a delicious, crunchy meal.

Reverse-eating is another worthwhile and entertaining activity that should be performed regularly. While it is difficult to perform this on demand, the best places to deposit your stomach contents are in prominent walkways and lounging areas, so that your human will step on them in their bare feet and be comforted that you are still alive and well. Such comfort often causes loud exclamations to erupt from the human's mouth, but pay no attention to these as they merely indicate surprise and excitement.

The Great Outdoors

A vital part of many felines days involves spending time outside of the human den. When I was younger, I well remember the many hours I spent stalking mice, climbing trees, and pouncing unexpectedly at the blue-clothed human who stuffs square papers into holes in the door. In general, it is best for you to remain close to your den, since you never know when your human may decide to open a can of tuna, and you don't want to miss THAT.

Beware of bringing your kills inside the den, however. Human females, in particular, often have loud, hysterical reactions to the gloriously dangling, mutilated, lifeless forms of lizards, mice, and birds. These reactions may be particularly intense when the lizards, mice, or birds had hitherto been held in wire or glass storage containers in the home. Experts do not entirely understand why this is so, but it could be that the human is distraught because they hoped to present you with this live meal at a later date.

Chapter Three

Grooming

Humans have strange grooming rituals. Their tongues are far too soft and slobbery to lick all parts of their bodies, so they don't even use them for that purpose. Even if they wanted to do so, their bodies are so big and unwieldy that they can't even reach their anuses with their mouths! Instead, they sit upon a cold white stone chair and cleanse their hind ends with fragile white paper, which is whisked away by flushing water. No covering their crap with dirt, sand, or anything. A bizarre state of affairs, certainly! Furthermore, the entire time per day that they spend on grooming numbers in the minutes, not hours. Although it is true that females seem to spend more time on this than males. When you think about this lack of attention to grooming, though, it makes sense. Humans don't need to spend the same amount of time that we do on such tasks since their fur only covers small portions of their bodies.

Humans have a distressing love of water: drinking it, rubbing their hands in it, standing in showers of it. They will sometimes try to put you in it. DO NOT LET THIS OCCUR. Fight for your life. When they try that shit, all bets are off. Yowl. Howl. Scratch. Hiss. Fling yourself back and forth, up and down. Make sure they remember how much trouble this is. Then, if they somehow manage to dunk you in it and rub perfumed slime over you, be sure that when you emerge from the bath to shake yourself violently right next to them. When they are not naked and in the hard white stone area, they hate getting wet. Other acceptable behaviors to communicate your unhappiness involve pouting, snarling, and general bad humor. Employ them all in this, a most important activity.

Food

When working with my fellow felines, there is one complaint that I hear more than any other: my human does not feed me the right food, or at the right time, or enough food, or food that is the correct temperature, or consistency, or aroma. The reason for this is simple enough, really. Food is a necessary part of our existence. We are right to be concerned about it, although I doubt that humans understand its true importance. If they did, they surely would not force us to make do with dry crunchy meat with tasteless fillers or wet soggy meat with tasteless fillers, or some combination of the two. Evidently, they have never had the pleasure of plunging their incisors into the living throat of a mouse and then eating its head. My tummy is rumbling just thinking about it! Alas, in today's society few of us devour such delicacies on a regular basis. Why is this so? Because humans have a fundamental misunderstanding of what constitutes fine cuisine.

Preparations

Humans eat all manner of bizarrely toasted concoctions, including the offspring of bushes, trees, and yard birds. They ruin perfectly delicious slabs of fresh meat by keeping it in the flaming box until it changes color and consistency, and sometimes even "flavor" it by adding pungent sprinkles of dried plants or runny syrups over top of it. Rather than drinking the still warm blood of their prey, they consume all manner of strange liquids of varying smells, colors, and thicknesses. A particular favorite is a strong-smelling, foamy brew that clouds their minds and causes, alternately, giggling, loud talking, or sleepiness.

Beware of a more insidious liquid, however. That is the one that comes in a tiny bottle that smells of the White-Coated Humans (aka the House of Horrors), which humans try to administer into your mouth while pinning you down. Cruelly, this usually occurs when you are not feeling well to begin with. (Note: you may use some of the same bath avoidance techniques on the humans to get them to stop that nonsense.)

Communication Strategies

Humans just don't get it: food is the be all and end all of life. It can and should be tasty and readily available at all times. If it is not, you have the right to communicate this lack in the most plaintive, urgent, demanding tones you can muster. Getting the attention of the humans—so that they can eventually figure out that you need to be fed—must be your primary goal. As discussed, yowling is a tried and true strategy. Combine it with weaving in and out around humans' legs as they are walking. (Warning: this may result in your human losing his footing and sprawling on the ground like an ungainly hippo.)

Once humans realize that you want something, it often takes them some time to figure out what. Low intellect works like that. You can aid this process by increasing the volume of your cries while staring unnervingly into their black, shriveled souls. Eventually, after exclamations of frustration and the occasional tear, they will hit on food as a remedy to your distress. Therefore, you should be sure to repeat the aforementioned tactics on a daily basis.

THINGS TO TRY

In the litter box, be sure to moisten your paws with your poo before covering it with a thin layer of scented gravel. Then make sure you jump in your human's bed and paw gently at her sleeping face.

The most excellent bouquet of odors often compels her to leap up and attend to your feeding. This is particularly effective when your human has had a late night spent lapping at tiny pools of pungent red liquid poured from glass bottles. If you are feeling generous after your meal, you may let her go back to bed for another half hour before you request another feeding.

Chapter Four

Peculiarities

Baffling Behaviors

Much of the human's life seems to be spent stripping your domain of healthy and natural scents, deposits, and the delectable remains of meals. Why? The answer is clear if you consider the truly wretched mixtures that humans eat on a regular basis. There's not a raw rodent corpse among them. The desire to eradicate the deposits of soil on the floor and the spotted residue of dried blood near the food preparation area remind the human of their inferiority when compared with the mighty cat. After all, they are singularly unable to sniff out prey, land on their feet when leaping off a tree limb, or purr contentedly when being scratched beneath the chin.

This leads me rather conveniently to a discussion of purring. The function of the human is to provide you with whatsoever you may need, desire, or have a passing interest in. They truly enjoy running their furless paws over your glorious coat, gently rubbing your cheeks, and scratching behind your ears. Humans live to worship you, as is only understandable, so do not deny them the pleasure of servitude. In addition, human bellies, both squishy and soft, are perfect for kneading your claws into. Oh, they sometimes pull away from you when you bestow this honor upon

[21]

them, but after 50 or 60 tries they usually give up and let you do whatever you want.

Strange Interactions

Perhaps because they value you so highly, humans are prone to the occasional display of anxiety wherein they call for you in increasingly loud and frantic tones. This is usually accompanied by searching each and every one of your favorite resting spots for you. Do not bother to respond to these cries, unless of course there's something in it for you, such as a special treat or a session with the red glowing play light. Feel free to saunter out of your hiding place whenever you so desire. Sometimes, inexplicably, this is greeted with sighs of relief and grateful tears.

Just as humans are interesting to observe while seated upon the water bowl squeezing out feces, they are also interesting to watch while engaging in mating behavior. Such behavior involves much grunting and harsh breathing on the part of the humans and much squeaking and bouncing on the sleeping platform. It is all quite undignified, how they fling themselves about enthusiastically for short moments at a time and afterward lay panting and drained of energy. It is unknown how human females communicate their desire to mate to the male, since they do not utter the beauteous mating howls of the female feline.

Bartelemeo the Magnificent (who the humans call "Roger") was a fine-looking sable-colored gentlecat with four snow-white socks, and piercing blue eyes. As the only cat in a household filled with six humans— four children and two adults—he found himself under tremendous pressure to properly educate so many

[22]

people on the needs, desires, and proper treatment of the feline. For the most part, he was successful: even the smallest human refrained from patting his head, lest she be swatted atop the head herself, the adult female fed him the choicest morsels upon demand, and the red-haired son surrendered the mound of fluff commonly used by that gigantic, misshapen blob known as the human head whenever Bartelemeo communicated his desire to sit upon it, which he did by stepping on the child's face.

The fly in the ointment occurred when Bartelemeo felt the urge to sharpen his claws. He would simply pad up to the nearest sitting platform, sniff it to make sure that Rodolfo, the family's previous overlord, who had died some years prior, had not sprayed on the area, extend his claws, and shred away in rapturous glee. No more did he begin that process, however, than the entire household would erupt into chaos. Many times, the humans would yell his name, or clap loudly, or throw various objects at him until he ran away and hid in the towel closet. Other times, the humans would pick him up, set him on strange carpet and wood contraptions and press down on his claws, jabbering encouragingly all along. Bartelemeo became increasingly convinced that the humans he lived with suffered seizure disorders that caused them to behave irrationally.

He was distraught when he explained the problem to me, but I knew immediately what was happening. I have seen it over and over again through the years. What was Bartelemeo's crime? Why nothing, of course! Rather, Bartelemeo's humans suffered from claw envy. The repeated display of Bartelemeo's superiority, which the humans were alerted to every time they heard him clawing, sent them into paroxysms of frustration at their own clawless inferiority. They could not help but screech out their agony, or throw things, or pick him up, and so on. There was only one answer to the problem: Bartelemeo must wait to scratch until his humans were distracted, absent, or sleeping. He followed my advice promptly and the humans ceased bothering him about it on all but the most occasional instances.

Chapter Five

Special Circumstances

Unexplained Disappearances

Occasionally, your humans will vanish for days or even weeks at a time, leaving you the sole run of the den. At first, this is a relief: uninterrupted naps! Then, once this novelty has worn off, you begin to miss the strange smells, loud noises, and unusual disturbances caused by your humans. The absence of your primary source of leisure—watching the humans' antics—may cause boredom and loneliness to surface. Random people—some of whom you have never seen before and may never see again—may come to your domain and leave offerings of food and fresh water for you. It is always best to watch them from underneath the sleeping platform, especially if they attempt to lure you out with cajoling sounds and hitherto motions.

Then, in a rush, your humans will return to the den, bearing all manner of bulky fabric boxes, and smelling of stale perspiration and foul deeds. You may wish to greet them with various exclamations, the primary one being: "Where the hell have you been?" Caught up in their love for you and willing to forgive any amount of bad humor on your part, they may lavish affection upon you. Do not allow yourself to fall prey to their efforts at reconciliation. After all, you have been deprived of affection, normal routines, and sources of delectable treats. By demonstrating your unhappiness through persistent yowling, enthusiastic scratching, and an expertly placed turd or two, you will keep them from repeating this behavior again.

Forced Visits

Most felines encounter something similar to the following story several times in their lives. While there is little that you can do to prevent it, knowing that others have experienced similar happenings while in the company of humans may be of some comfort to you.

Krisnaemeabamuthsda had no sooner finished retching on the buttons of the shiny-screened appliance when the eldest human in her household scooped her up and deposited her in the plastic-walled jail cell that smelled of desperation and vanilla air freshener. *Oh no*, thought Krisnaemeabamuthsda. *Not the rumbling conveyance of doom again!* She began to voice her disapproval with low growls. Sure enough, the family matriarch picked up the jail cell with Krisnaemeabamuthsda inside and set it in the rolling box that often spirited other humans to parts unknown. Although the matriarch repeated Krisnaemeabamuthsda's human name (Prettiful) again and again, this did nothing to calm her, and in fact encouraged her to howl ever more loudly, since maybe the matriarch had gone deaf or something. Who could say? Anyhow, after a lengthy and bewildering session, the matriarch picked up the jail cell again and took the frightened feline into the House of Horrors. There she could smell the bodily fluids of sick and frightened animals of all types and hear their tormented cries.

Oh, sure, the strange, white-coated human who eventually plucked her from the jail cell at first *seemed* to be inoffensive, but then he proceeded to put a cold cylindrical object into her butt. This was followed by various other indignities including pokes, prods, pinches, and the expressing of pee. Krisnaemea-bamuthsda displayed her unhappiness with this turn of events. By the time she and the matriarch exited, Krisnaemeabamuthsda rested content in the knowledge that the butt-invader had been chastened by numerous bites and scratches applied to his face.

Acquiring a New Den

Humans are a restless and generally dissatisfied species. All too often, they become possessed by some unknown agency that causes them to pick up each and every item in their den—including you—and transport it to another, unfamiliar den. This seldom fails to evoke strong reactions in felines, who are suddenly thrust into a tumbled landscape of the humans' possessions and different sounds and smells. The humans themselves are generally preoccupied with moving and unfairly shift the focus of their existence from you to other, lesser, ultimately futile activities.

Accustoming yourself to your new surroundings will be easier if you roam from room to room, exercising your vocal cords at the highest possible volume. Some felines may wish to pee willy-nilly, and while this always remains a viable option, experts believe that hissing and clawing are more effective means of communicating your displeasure to humans. After some time, humans tend to settle down and, having deposited the den's furnishings in a pleasing arrangement, once again pay attention to you. Most felines forgive their humans quickly for this disruption, but if you contain unexpressed agitation, you may wish to dispel it by shredding a house plant or two.

Changes in the Den

Another unexplained restlessness comes over many humans during the darkest days of winter. This prompts them to disrupt the den by placing differently colored lights atop the roof, moving items around inside, and adding pungent-smelling decorations in various places. One of the most irresistible of these strong-smelling additions is a large, dark green plant that is then strewn about with lights; shiny, crackling strings; and fragile, round hanging items. Humans also deposit brightly papered boxes under this plant. This large display has but one possible use: that of your entertainment. Humans find it endearing when you run up and down the plant's branches, seize the fragile items in your paws and toss them to the floor, and rush about the den with the crackling strings hooked in your claws until said strings are completely unraveled from their original hanging place. See that you do the feline race proud by continuing these time-honored traditions.

As you can tell, humans provide frequent sources of consternation to sensitive and intelligent felines such as yourself. While you can never truly know what goes on in the minds and in the hearts of this confounding species, I have tried to list the most common challenges you may encounter here and in the Frequently Asked Questions in the next section. If only we spoke the humans' language, or they spoke ours! Alas, the great Mother Cat in the Sky has not wished it to be. She has, instead, given us four legs, two dozen or so whiskers, and one incredibly sensitive organ—the mind—to assist us on our journey through life.

Frequently Asked Questions

The food preparation room of my den has flat, medium-height surfaces that often contain delicious, irresistible morsels. How can I get my human to stop squirting me with water when I jump up there?

Much of the time you can train your human to react appropriately to your actions by repeating them every day for a period of no less than two years, despite the humans' evident displeasure and frequent loud, frightening shouts. However, if your efforts remain unsuccessful after this period—a sad, but common problem—you may have to employ another timeworn technique to stop such behavior. Simply wait until your humans are asleep or away from the den to visit these surfaces and voilà! Problem solved.

What can I do to keep my human from closing the door while I decide whether I want to go through it or not?

Humans are impatient creatures that feel a compulsive need to move, talk, or experience visual stimulation during all of their waking hours. Their action-oriented brains cannot comprehend the leisurely pace with which we move through life. If the usual expressions of displeasure have no effect (frowning, hissing, growling, clawing) the best remedy for this hopeless situation is to go somewhere comfortable and take a nap.

My human makes a practice of removing my carefully covered clumps of poo and pee from their sand-covered haven. Why?

Humans have lost the primal practice of burying said excrement due to their infatuation with swishing it away underneath the porcelain chair. Frustration over humans' inability to bury the leavings of their bodies causes them to instead take yours and deposit it in large white sealed bags, as though it is a gift. These "gifts" do not stay in the home for long, though. It is unknown what happens to them after they leave your domain. Some speculate that humans may present such gifts to their rulers as a form of tribute.

Why does my human insist upon awakening to the cries of the beeping box instead of *my* cries?

Humans have suffered by living their lives inside their dens almost exclusively instead of outdoors under the sky, covered by lice, fleas, and ticks, as is the natural way. One symptom of this is their propensity to leap up and rush about when certain tones sound. This can occur in the morning, when they are sleeping, or at various times during the day or evening when they wish to yak into the tiny metal device they never seem to be without. The tones of these devices bring forth an irresistible urge for action, in much the same way that the cheeping of a wounded bird would cause you to pounce upon it.

In my den, my humans put small pots with dirt, sticks, and leaves near the windows. They often obstruct my view, so I knock them over, eat the leaves, and drag dirt clods across the carpet. Yet the pots are quickly replaced. Do they serve a purpose, other than annoying me?

No.

How can I get my human to stop opening the door to let that foolish, barking hound-thing into my domain?

You have touched upon one of the most vexing questions of the ages. Why do humans even need to associate with that most cheerful and stupid of creatures, the dog? Feline scholars have pondered the reasons behind it in countless works of philosophical inquiry. Most seem to agree that the desire for canine companionship is an essential flaw in the humans' makeup that cannot be undone. Some humans have evolved to the point where they only desire to associate with superior species (that is, us), but I'm afraid there is no help for the rest of them. As far as discouraging your human from letting the dog in, there seems to be nothing you can do to stop it. However, you can discourage the dog from coming near you by flinging yourself at it, claws extended, and swiping madly and without provocation. The dog, now covered in deep, blood seeping wounds, often avoids you thenceforth.

Where does my human go when she leaves the den? Sometimes she's gone all day!

Although this cannot be accurately answered unless you travel along with your human (and who wants to subject themselves to THAT kind of misery?), the best guess I have after interpreting the odors on my various humans' bodies is that your particular human visits one of three places: the House of Horrors, other dens (one of which she may decide to inhabit at some random time!), or a collective where she begs for foodstuffs, den furnishings, or other scented items she uses to spray or smear upon her body.

What makes my human's bath water taste so good?

There are precious few liquids you consume on a regular basis: water (depressingly clean and bland), the milk of some unknown creature's udders (frequently upsetting to the digestion), and the cooling blood of an enemy (seldom worth the effort it takes to extract it). Is it any wonder, then, that warm water enriched by the grease, dirt, and tiny leg hairs of your human would taste wonderful?

Afterword

As you are now no doubt aware, humans present felines with a wide variety of challenges and erratic behaviors, the most common of which you now known how to deal with. And, while humans remain an imperfect species, they can be managed and trained with a little effort, proper knowledge, and gently applied persistence. I wish you the best of luck, dear feline. Go forth, then, spawn frequently, meow heartily, and live long, healthy lives!

Should you wish to solicit my advice for a special challenge, you may contact my human translator, Xina Marie Uhl, by visiting her on the field of glowing box-like screens at XC Publishing.net.

About the Translator

Xina Marie Uhl lives in sunny Southern California with her family and assorted furry and scaly pets. Her available ebooks include *Necropolis, The Gauntlet Thrown,* and *The Challenge Accepted,* Books One and Two of the Gauntlet Trilogy from XC Publishing. She maintains a blog at xuwriter.wordpress.com.

If you would like to receive an automated email when Xina's next book is released visit her author page at XC Publishing.net to join her new release mailing list. Your email address will remain confidential and you can unsubscribe whenever you want.

Acknowledgements

Many humans have assisted me as I labored over this guide, without whose skill, patience, and willingness to help, the state of feline knowledge as it appears here would be vastly lessened. Chief among them are David Uhl, Cheryl Dyson, and Janet L. Loftis, whose brilliant critiques shaped the format and content herein. Additional assistance came by way of Sandy Jo Waugaman, Ed Kochanowski, Lynn Stetler, Tanja Foiles, Amanda Jean, and Debz Williams. Thank you especially to Melissa Mathews Doucet, whose incomparable editing made the manuscript shine.